OCR A2
Economics

Peter Smith

OCR A2
Economics

Peter Smith

Philip Allan, an imprint of Hodder Education, an Hachette UK company, Market Place, Deddington, Oxfordshire OX15 0SE

Orders

Bookpoint Ltd, 130 Milton Park, Abingdon, Oxfordshire OX14 4SB
tel: 01235 827827
fax: 01235 400401
e-mail: education@bookpoint.co.uk
Lines are open 9.00 a.m.–5.00 p.m., Monday to Saturday, with a 24-hour message answering service. You can also order through the Philip Allan Updates website: www.philipallan.co.uk

ISBN 978-1-4441-9550-7

First published 2009
Second edition 2013

Impression number   5 4 3 2 1
Year   2017 2016 2015 2014 2013

All website addresses included in this book are correct at the time of going to press but may subsequently change.

All photographs are reproduced by permission of Topfoto, except where otherwise specified.

Printed in Dubai

Hachette UK's policy is to use papers that are natural, renewable and recyclable products and made from wood grown in sustainable forests. The logging and manufacturing processes are expected to conform to the environmental regulations of the country of origin.

P02252